POEMS OF THE
Heart

DURIME P. ZHERKA

authorHOUSE®

AuthorHouse™
1663 Liberty Drive
Bloomington, IN 47403
www.authorhouse.com
Phone: 1 (800) 839-8640

Published by AuthorHouse   03/08/2016

ISBN: 978-1-5049-8346-4 (sc)
ISBN: 978-1-5049-8345-7 (e)

Library of Congress Control Number: 2016903830

CONTENTS

1 Flowwer and Butterfly!

One peaceful day
The sun was shining
With its gold color
And all the beautiful flowers
Were brighting more.
One butterfly was flying around
To one lonely flower
With its wing touched
The petals that were down to the green field
Started one sparkling conversation between them.
Why you beautiful flower are so sad?
Why your petals are down to the earth?
Who did not like your nectar in this filed
And makes you desperate in deep.
I am your butterfly that I love you
And sun is shining you,
also the trees are and birds
are looking and greeting you,
so in this world are others that love you.

2 You and Nature.!

With spring time almost here

I feel myself with full desire

Your sweet words to hear

About our great love.

I see you are coming through

The green fields

With a lot flowers in your hand

And the wind is playing crazy

With your beautiful and long hair.

I saw your smile

that is appearing out of your teeth

like white pearls

and melody of your song

was spreading happiness everywhere.

You and this colorful nature are so beautiful in my eyes.

Both of you are giving full love in my heart.

3

Immigrant

I traveled around the world from east to west.
I saw everywhere you immigrant
To fight for progress.
Always your sublime sacrifice
between life and die it is strong fighting,
between dark and light.
From undeveloped world,
Where is suffering everyone
To developed world where is big light.,
You need to escape a stronger border desert and hills,
And sea and ocean,
Your dreams and hopes
For more better life
In your golden heart
always will win to you immigrant

I am waiting!

I am waiting the strange day

To see again you

at a given moment in my life.

I am waiting the wonderful time

To talk with you

And to put some peace in my mind.

I am waiting synchronicity

Of our thoughts to rise

As all elements of new life cycle

Are arranged for us.

I am waiting by the time

That my wish and hope to become true

And to put our feelings in resonance.

I am waiting all these to happen in my future life

And to be happy with you.

I am waiting, I am waiting too!

5 What will be!

In this beautiful evening
The moon and stars are so bright.
I am thinking about
Our story has been started.
Can it be a strong friendship
With honesty and loyalty
As everyone in life needs?
Can it be a big beginning
Of a love story with a full meaning?
I need answer for my question.
I sent it to constellation.
The beautiful stars with full moon
started their argue about you and me.
Our relationship what will be?
All of them sent to me l
Like "Excuse" signals light
They need time to decide.
I thanks them for cooperation.
I will use patience
To take answer from constellation
about you and me,
our relationship what will be?

Hurting of my feelings!

I tried to created barrier
To this flood of thoughts
In my mind,
That follow me everywhere,
Every time,
While does not leave me quiet.
I wanted to forget our strong argue last time,
To give your mind some light.
I wrote to you one letter,
My feelings were hot.
I thought "Our storm"
Was going with flow,
While your answer sent to me
One mountain with snow.
The reason of your changing,
Never I know
But hurting of my feelings
Never can go.
I am trying to help myself
In this difficult time,
Well known medicine is
To get you out of my mind.

Race Of Animals

A noise is coming from forest
Suddenly the birds flied
Out of the trees.
The sheep were going away.
from this noise to be faraway.
The king Lion came with powerful view,
One fox said with jealousy,
As important animal
You must count and me,
One tiger laughed with irony,
And gave greeting to elephantine.
The Eagle nervous about this view
Flied faraway to ocean blue.
Sharks and alligators started swimming fast
and said, nobody can ignore us.
Horses, gamiles, thought strangely,
this field only our job needs.
The trees, corns and flowers said
In this place we are powerful we
We are making this nature very beautiful.

8 Seasons

As wedding dressing
The snow covers mountains
Its silver light is brighting by the sun,
The trees looks tired
And complained to wild winter,
the time with you is going long run.
We are going to spring time.
When the snow was coming
down and rivers water came up
and the fields dressed with green grass,
the song of the birds were telling
for spring time,
while nature and people were in love.
When green color was changing to yellow,
and sun was hot,
lovely summer time said
with me people will have fun.
When is raining with wind
And leaves were coming down
autumn time said
People need me to be some quiet.

Garden of Oranges.

Do you remember
Our beautiful garden
Full with oranges
Your expressing of love
To me was very strange.
The green color of trees
Campaigned with orange color
Created a beautiful frame
Of our love story.
I am walking now through
To our beautiful garden
Full with oranges and my memories
Are bringing to my mind
Your love with full faith.
Under this roof of trees
With bright green
And orange color.
We started our wonderful love story
In our beautiful garden
The sun was shining capricious
Our love and oranges were delicious.

Tirana

O beautiful Tirana
Your wonderful view
Appears in front of me
Is awaking my feelings
That for along time are sleeping,
To fly free.
Your beautiful buildings
That rivals to the sky
Very strong and hard
To your street like arterial,
Are giving life's blood
To your heart.
With their green colors hills
Like circle around you,
Looks are defending
A water of lake blue.
In this beautiful place
With flowers multicolor,
I spent my youngest time,
So fun with friend of mine.
In my memories,
my life belongs to you
From bottom of my heart
Tirana I love you.

Sterberda

Never I know who named you
Sterberda, before some hundred years,
But your romantic view
Is making me speechless.
Through the branches of the trees
The rays of the sun
are coming in hidden way,
With me they want to play.
When I am watching you
Sterberda my lovely hill
My mind has full peace
With your cover green.
In your beautiful forest
All the beautiful trees like in parada
Are creating a green roof under the sun
For flowers that are around.
The waters noise of one stream
Like symphony
Makes your nature very lovely.

12 Our songs

It was difficult time
For everything we asked why?
We were singing in illegal way
Our favorite Italian songs
"Che Sara" and "Partirai"
Their beautiful melody
Was spreading faraway
Through the Adriatic sea
Our hope for democracy.
In our beautiful Tirana
When it can't took breath
Our thought for the "West"
Were "Utopia" "Privilege"
When the wind of democracy
Everything for better changed
"Che sara" and "Partirai"
I never can forget.
Now I am faraway.
These songs are my memory
"Che Sara" and "Partirai"
Always will be
One solid bridge
Between you and me.

Flower of Jargavan!

It was the most happy day
For all of us in class
When teacher said strict
Today we are making lesson
To garden botanic.
During her explanation
Through this garden multicolor
For special of flowers in line
You gave to me one
Beautiful flower of Jargavan.
Your magical words
I love you
Came quickly to me
In my heart through
More fast than teacher's words
I need one personal herbarium
From every one of you.
Around me were flying up to the sky
Together with butterflies
The loudly words of teacher
For attention of everyone while
I was thinking for your lovely Jargavan.

Our dancing.

The Saturday evening
Was bringing happiness
When I prepared myself
To dance with you
Waltz "Danub Blue"
When orchestra started
Our Waltz "Danub Blue"
I felt myself that I was flying with you.
Suddenly the sounds
of this melody changed through
I started to dance
In hidden corner twist with you.
Strangely one friend said:
What is wrong with you,
this dance is prevented by law
It is not for you.
You must continue
With Waltz "Danub Blue"
With a lot restrictions
In my youngest time
Never they stopped me to love
others dancing through,
Never they stopped me to love you
The wonderful waltz "Danub Blue"

One Pelican!

Walking on the beach

Looking to ocean

Suddenly close to me came one pelican

It's head down to yellow sand

Was showing me that it was sad.

The white pelican looks so lonely

Maybe it was thinking for his friends like me.

After this moment came close to us,

Three more its friends

White Peilicans.

All of them with their noise,

Craw, craw, craw opened their wings

With happiness and charm

Were flying above the ocean.

I felt myself again lonely

On this sand light

Without friends of mine

Without the white pelican.

Like became together

The white pelicans,

So I want to be with friends of mine.

When I was with you!

When I was with you everything looks bright

My heart was glad,

My mind was light

Our conversations were lovely.

We did not know that existed

the strange word "Hypocrisy"

your situation is new for me

I do not see more to you clarity

It is scaring me your false smile

I do not see rain and sun

In your beautiful face

Like before.

While I liked this storm

In our beautiful time

I loved your "so sorry"

For mistakes were done,

I loved your honesty

I can't accept the new element

Between you and me

"Hypocrisy"

To save in my memory

Our purely love it is enough

I am leaving you,

OUT OF MY LIFE!

Welcome Spring Time.

The gray color of weather
Capricious wants to stay
From mountain to the field faraway.
The trees complained to winter we are so tired
With you is going a long time
We are going to spring time.
The green color strongly
Covered the field
while the white flowers,
were showing happiness
for green color friends to be.
The trees as loyal friends
Of the filed are filling their branches
With green leaves.
Children that are enjoying this field,
Are playing with cheer,
The sun is watching view, it thought,
They need my warm and light,
to say welcome spring time.

Parada in Tirane.

Dajti proudly is showing,
To "everyone", I am powerful in Tirane,
All the people, loves me
For my fresh air and forest green,
With their mansion beautiful,
they are doing my view wonderful.
The hill with lake blue
Said here I am beautiful,
For my lake and garden botanic
A lot people are making picnic
The modern buildings
Are going high, said
we are beauty in Tirana's heart,
For our gray and blue glass,
all people love us.
The wide and long boulevard
Is showing his pride
With my classic buildings,
I am important here,
I represent culture and science.
The "Skenderbeu" square said:
Without me.
Where young people fought for democracy
You never will have your "Beauty"

Our friendship

We promised each other
During hard time
Our friendship to be alive.
How much we dreamed
If democracy will arrive
for more happy life
When we suffered both of us
For unreasonable reasons
For because a lot because…!!!
Their explanations never knows.
Was going a long time
Of our promises in Tirane.
Now are destiny is decided
Again our friendship is alive
From each other we are faraway.
Our strongly friendship
Is continuing same way.
Weeks, months, years
Are sending to me
Your love every time,
Through mountains and ocean
I am happy for you friend of mine.

The moment has come.

Through the wide and green
In your hand a lot flowers I see.
While you are coming to me
With your question and option
about my choice of flowers,
with different forms and colors.
You bring to me with your action
Your joy and satisfaction
That created to me
full happiness as reaction.
The moment has come to me
to show to you my deep feelings
For my choice really true
About the most beautiful
flower and you.
This choice is difficult for me.
I feel; as I thought you and flower
Are in perfect harmony
And the moment has come for me,
me to tell you,
How much I love you!

I Am Thinking.

On my garden with flowers
Sitting under tree
In this beautiful day
I am thinking for you.
While the branches of the trees
Are sending to me
Like illegal way
The warm of sun's rays
And my memories
are making awake.
My thoughts are flying
to you faraway
And are creating a beautiful
Image of your face.
Your smile is making me warm
Like sun's ray.
I am thinking for you in silence
while I am asking myself
Are you thinking for me
In this beautiful day
with hot feelings in same way.

Albanian's Riviera.

The line of the hills
Are dressing their green
And yellow colors
While are showing to everyone
Their delicious fruits
Oranges and lemons.
In this flora community
Members are and olives trees.
Down to the beautiful hills
The long way is campaigned
The line of beach faraway,
With its water very blue.
The sea Jon is creating
with its waves the fresh air.
With their white color and red roofs,
The houses looks beautiful
Are making this view wonderful.
All this mosaic color green
Blue yellow, red and white
Are lighting by warm sun
for everyone,
You are named
beautiful Perla
Albanian's Riviera.

Our rock in the blue" Jon" sea

Sitting alone in our rock

In the blue "Jon" sea.

I am watching the horizon

Where the grey color of the sky

Is kissing the blue color of the Jon" sea.

Blue and grey created one line

on extra ordinary vision

Suddenly flooded in my mind.

I dreamed like in depth

Of the night,

while our love story

appears in front of me.

When we together were sitting

On the rock in the blue" Jon "sea

Were talking and laughing lovely

While the waves capricious

Made noise around you and me.

I am sitting alone on our lovely rock

In the blue "Jon" sea,

Now that you are not with me

Under the hot sun

I am enjoying my memory

With juice vision

Of our love story.

The Beautiful Fort Lauderdale.

Invisible power
Activated my energy
Fort Lauderdale to write for you.
Through the street under the trees
My eyes are getting serenity
By your cover green.
Palmas proudly for their height
Are leaders in the long line
Of others trees and
All kind of flowers around
Suddenly the buildings capricious
In your heart are showing
Up to the sky their heads
With their blue glass,
Are creating magic mirror
For the warmer sun's rays.
Palmas trees, flowers and building
with their glass blue,
are giving me direction
to Ocean blue,
where the birds
Are flying, like a big crew.
The people's happiness
Is everywhere, you are
so beautiful Fort Lauderdale.

25

Hidden feelings.

Some hidden feelings
Are playing to us.
They want to come out
And going back fast.
This situation back and come
Makes our conversation very hot.
We are talking together
About different things
But eyes and heart
Are expressing the others feelings.
I am watching you and
Your expression face,
Your words and mine
In your voice's vibration
Low and up
I want to discover
The hidden feelings
That makes very warm my heart.
I am thinking and dreaming
I am waiting one sweet word
From our hidden feelings.
I am trying to make barrier
But always they are winning.

Your reaction.

It is going some times
When really I started
To think about you
Every day I was dreaming
About you and me
My thoughts to be reality
From your heart with hot feelings
Your lovely words
To come to me.
I think and I hope
But your reaction
Cold and warm
I can't afford.
It makes me confuse
About my thoughts
I want to express my thoughts
I want to express my love.
Form your heart I need support,
But your reaction
Cold and warm
Is hurting my love that is new born.
More clarity your behavior
My love will be warm.

The white Cloud.

The rain of weather grey
Campaigned by my tears
Makes both my feelings
And weather more cold and grey.
The clouds that are moving fast
Looks with my soul are in resonance.
One white cloud came down to me,
said a lot tears in your eyes I see.
I am ambassador from sky grey
My mission will be,
Your soul from sadness
To make free.
With my color very white.
I am bringing peace in your heart.
I am bringing one message bright.
The Universe is opening for you
The green light.
Suddenly in horizon faraway
Are coming some sun' rays
With their smile
They looks and said
With our golden and color bright
We are erasing
The blue color from your life.

I want to know.

I want to know
What do you think for me
While I am suffering one
Battle inside that my feelings
To put hidden or to make free.
I want to know
What do you think for me…?
While some invisible barriers
Created by your communication
Are stopping me.
Is it open the big way
In your heart to enter
My feelings very hot?
Is it going a clear idea
In your thoughts through
That my love for you
it is strong and very true.
I want to know
What do you think for me…?
I want to put my love
In the other heart
with full security
I want to bridge forever, lovely
Feelings between you and me.

I am waiting your answer

I am waiting your answer
For a long time in alert
Are acceptors of my mind
For your answer to get signal
And to send to my heart
For my love the great question
That has never been answered to me
Makes it running wild today
my creative energy.
Your answer is coming to me
in different ways,
that makes to feel myself close to you,
sometimes or to stay faraway.
I am waiting good answer
With time, so my love will grow up
strongly in my heart and in my mind.
I am waiting your good answer
To brings happiness to me
As a confirmation of a hidden
Love that need some
light between you and me.

My letters.

I sent a lot letters to you
I am not sure
I stamped my feelings
In white letters and black ink
if you have reading them through
that every moment of happiness
or worries of my daily life
for you think.
I am about to tell you
May surprise and even shock you,
all the time I am thinking for you
all those letters are holding
the weighting of my feelings
and all the time that I am thinking.
The letters that I sent to you
Our communication makes alive
in a good or bad time
They are loyal friends of mine.
This transmission bridge
During this period time
Wit storm weather and sun
Has value for love and for fun.

June's Time.

It was June's time when all
The exams were in line.
I was reading and thinking
With you in my mind was one
Happy and difficult time.
Outside latter night I heard
Gjinkallat with their noise
Zhu, zhu zhu, in interference
I heard it was one
whispering for you.
one small stone knocked
window,
I was happy for you
And scared from my mother too!
Her strong voice came to me
Later night,
What is happening with you?
Why window is opened
and curtains are moving too?
Dear mother I am listening,
Gjinkallat and the wind by the
window came through.

I was happy when she left
I wanted to talk with you
I was forgetting the exams
were coming,
I was listening
You and Gjinkallat,
Zhu, zhu, zhu,
Zhu, zhu zhu

Our meeting.

I am counting days
I am counting weeks
The happy ties is coming
Each other to see.
I am preparing myself to say
A lot problems like water of sea
And to tell how important
you are for me,
Inside me like stream are
moving hot and strange
Feeling with curiosity
Our meeting how will be.
I am waiting this time
For me and you
to express my feelings true.
I want to erase
all the doubts of this time
With beautiful cover
of clearly and lovely
Thoughts in my mind.
I am waiting this day
I am waiting to see you
In our meeting my wishes
To come true.

Your Changing.

I am confuse about your behavior,
The doubt I have for you,
My heart have broken.
From childhood.
From childhood
we have one verdict,
nothing can broke
our strongly friendship.
I am thinking during this time
How much you changed
with me friend of mine?!
How much you makes
weakness our friendship,
That was growing up with love and clarity.
I do not want to know
Who put between us distance.
What I want to know
is to keep in my heart
our relationship to be alive
and why in our life
we faced good or bad things,
we must to save our golden promises
about our loyalty friendship.

Difficult Language!

You spoke so much
With difficult terms
Your speech was fluently,
For me all words were same.
I liked your style
of your conversation
But never I understood
your expression.
I thought maybe you spoke
for Science – Convention.
I asked myself in silence
If you can find in this world
More simple words.
When you are talking with me,
To please in your office
leave your terminology.
I need to hear more simple words,
That are coming from your heart,
That are making our communication
very light.
Our conversation
is not for Convention
About speech of art.
It is the bridge
to put a strong connection
in our hearts.

My Defense.

Via mail Paris – Tirane for you
Was full with letters of mine.
Your returning showed me
Our sweet words like before
for our love,
erased by theory of physic nuclear.
I heard, I waited, I hoped,
The words of love,
from your heart to come through
and our dream to become true.
I was happy for your passion,
About new profession.
I was sad for our love,
Stole by Protons and electrons,
your question to me
as important part of your life
and your dream
about experience Paris – Tirane.
For physic nuclear.
I gave defence for the corns
and the field as agriculture specialist,
from you and your orbit
with radioactivity,
I want to be electron free.

Friend of mine.

Together we fought for democracy,

For more better life in our country.

Strangely the luck decided our places.

You in London and me in U. S.

I was dreaming in my memories

for our friendship between you and me.

Suddenly tring, tring the phone rings

Interrupted my dream.

My heart gave happy signal to my mind.

It is phone rings of friend of mine.

Through the long bridge

Of the blue water of Ocean,

That waves that are dancing with pelicans,

Are bringing to me in every sadness

moments and happy time,

The phone rings of friend of mine.

Every days news richest people big properties,

I read, I think, I laugh,

I feel myself strong and rich.

I have big gold's mine,

because I have Ani friend of mine.

You undermined me!

Along time inside myself,

I had one doubt for our friendship.

There were not mistakes,

But with your conscience

You undermined me.

Your behavior made cold my heart,

It is not easy to force me smile.

No matter where are you.

I feel reassure and completely calm,

While as clear as crystal

I see my feelings are sparkling light.

And why you had hurt me dramatically.

And prevented me at all.

Now the stars brilliantly

Are shining for me.

I will accomplish my goal.

I feel secure of myself and

I will be able to take a deep breath.

Conversation's Colors!

Painful memories that are in my head
are causing the certain degree of melancholy.
While never I understood your feelings for me.
Your conversation dressed different colors
And made my soul in terror.
Some times your words
were covered with strongly color blue,
that made me unsecure,
with sweet feelings of harmony.
In our conversation was coming color pink,
Suddenly the fire of love gave sign alert
and campaigned with color red.
I was terrifying from all those colors
with interference.
I gave to my heart and my mind,
from you the moments of silence.
I like in nature the rainbow with multi colors
but not in our love story.

The Beach of Adriatic Sea!

The long line of the beach
Of the blue Adriatic sea
Is in the world the most
Wonderful view that
Albania can be proud too.
The blue color of the sea
From the white waves
Taking garniture light to grey,
From the wind is going up to the hills
To meet color green
And a lot monuments historic
That are making this beach
Very interesting.
The trees that are watching
This panorama beautiful
around the hills at all
are creating one green
frame like honor,
between the hills and all
are creating one green
frame like honor.
Between the hills and Adriatic sea
In harmony the beautiful houses
And fields with flowers
Everyone can see.

Kosovo's Flowers.

By the dark thoughts of the people
with their head very hot,
the flowers covered
all around the field
as honor of the blood of martyrs.
I am remembering now in silence
Albanian people in Kosovo
with their eyes full with tears
that thought that lost their dreams,
while hope for life gave to them
the missioners of Peace.
Now that you Kosovo
are changing fast,
these flowers are
giving to you the color of life.
Kosovo is your duty to spread
Around the world this life's color
To erase forever the dark of the war.

The Wolf and Sheep!

One beautiful and sunny day,
The trees were witnesses
Of the strange conversation
Between wolf and one sheep
That were drinking water
to one stream of the hill,
through the clear water
of the stream
were moving cloudy and
bad thoughts of the wolf
for the sheep.
The wolf stayed on the top of the hill
While said you are doing mixer
the water for me.
The honestly sheep that stayed
on the bottom of the hill said:
I understand you want me to eat.
With her broke heart
The quietly sheep understood
one rule one rule strict,
in this beautiful nature
with wild animals
never will have friendship.

Seven a clock at the evening!

Seven a clock at the evening,
When night opened her veil dark,
for our meeting I was running fast.
Together we tried to hidden
under the trees ourselves,
from the light of the street.
The moon was sending its light
Across the branches of the trees
And made our meeting very romantic.
While I laughed and I talked with you,
I thought seven a clock
Is lovely time for romantic meeting
as has everyone.
Every seven a clock at the evening
the lights of the street,
were giving direction to you.
Our lovely whispering under the tree,
Every time campaigned bright
By moon's silver light.

Bill Clinton with Kosovo's refugees!

Now you beautiful Kosovo

Are enjoying in freedom

your life,

your flowers are awaking

in my memory one difficult time,

when your people with tears,

that were going down to the faces,

and their broken hearts

were leaving their homes,

their land behind.

I saw Bill Clinton between

Albanian refugees from Kosovo

in Macedonia with his smile,

compassionate and wonderful words,

for them and for me,

that gave a full hope,

to those people that suffered

the terrible war.

Bill Clinton for your activity

against this war you have forever,

the Albanian people's heart as honor.

Tonny Blair in Tirana!

In beautiful Tirana
I saw you Tonny Blair
With your smile that gave
good impression to everyone.
I saw you clever man
between refugees of Kosovo
with your optimism and your energy
that you gave a full hope and
one wonderful dream
for Albanian people
that had their eyes full with tears.
From the terrible war
they were suffering.
Your speech very enthusiastic
Was putting in the hearts
of Albanian people life
one beautiful spring.
With your helping and activity,
You have forever the big love
And thank you from
Albanian people and from me.

George W. Bush in Tirana!

One beautiful day
when enthusiasm of the people
and sun was so light,
George W. Bush your presence
In Tirana for Albanian people
was their pride.
For Albania and Tirana was
a huge progress that visited
for the first time
by the president of the U. S.
With your smile, your meeting,
was lovely and warm.
Everyone wanted to meet,
to huge, to talk with you.
For your lovely visit
to my country too,
like my people I love you.
The people in Tirana were cheerful
And nature was so beautiful,
In this picture very lively
and colorful,
President George W. Bush,
your visit was so wonderful.

Spring Time!

I am happy today and I see,
that the beautiful flowers
and the birds with their songs
are happy like me.
I am walking in sidewalk
and I feel that proudly Palmas,
are looking to me,
they want to know
about my euphoria.
The green grass carpet
with his silence,
for my joyful has a big curiosity.
The golden sun with his rays
Is touching my skin
with jealousy.
With his provocative warm,
wants attention of me,
as always, winner of my feelings
he wants to be.
I love this nature that is
Giving hope to me,
How to live in harmony
with those that are close to me.
I am telling all of them secret of mine
Today I am in love with Spring time.

To be American!

To be American this is preposition phrase
With three gold words,
that is a big dream
for thousands people
around the world.
Everyone can ask you and me,
What is the meaning American to be?
To be American means
inspiration source for better life,
to give and to get love from the other side.
To help the poor people
on undeveloped world,
where the life is black and grey,
but are living people like you and me.
It is American duty to give his progress,
he is creating the big credit in Universe.
To be America means
to be soldier of the victory,
to give freedom to unprotected people
to change in this strange world
the ugly face of misery.
It means death of dictator
and growing the democracy's tree,
to ensure.
It is value like a brilliant for everyone
To hold name American.

Missioner of Peace

After those years everyone
Can see on facade crystal's memory
With gold color their name
of Albanian's people history as honor.
It appears the names
very lovely Bill Clinton and Tony Blair
as sensor of Peace everywhere.
With her insight and diplomacy
Madeleine Albright her name is shining
very light in Albanian's people history.
This time the color is coming more bright
with super star Michael Douglas
with big heart as symbol of peace
with his activity in Gramsh
in difficult case and time,
all Albanian people for him feel pride.
The beauty Nicole Kidman with her activity
She stamped her name
in Albanian people's history.

Sitting on the field!

Sitting on the field with green grass,
I am watching the flowers
that are blooming fast.
In this peaceful nature
I feel inside me the good energy
that may establish.
My thoughts in inner harmony
And brings to my life a lot happiness.
With their songs the birds are
flying on the field above the green grass
are making me faithful to my desires.
I am dreaming my life to be so beautiful
Like this nature also very peaceful.
Sitting on the field with green grass,
I forget my angry and anxiety.
I think my life very lovely
with everyone around me to be
in harmony like this wide field
with beautiful flowers and this grass green,
I want to be true for my life this dream.

My Love during Spring time!

The Trees looks are whispering
about our love.
When they are looking you and me
in this sunny day through our smiling,
they are understanding our happiness.
My heart is full with love
about this lovely nature.
My mind is in peace
in this wonderful view
when I am laying down on
the green grass under the sky blue,
and close with me are you.
The sun with his jealousy
Is sending to our eyes
his light,
our conversation to interrupt.
The lovely trees with their leaves
From sun's rays are defending our eyes.
I think I laugh,
I am listening your magical words of love,
That are coming to me like butterflies.
I think I am in love with spring time.

Marry with Me!

It was one autumn's day
When you said very lovely
Marry with me!
I listened your words carefully.
I felt reaction inside of me.
I felt at half of my body was cold.
My family and my friends I thought.
I was scared for my new life,
I will follow sometime.
I felt my body was hot
when your face I saw.
My heart was going fast
while in my hand I felt I had snow.
My answer to give to you never I know.
MARRY WITH ME!
It was simple phrase,
For my life was deep
and big changing,
and why this big conflict to my mind
it came through,
I loved this phrase and you too!

Beautiful Istanbul.

It Is a big surprise your
Interesting beauty that
appears in seven hills,
for everyone,
your mixer architecture
bizantin and European.
The famous bridge Bosphor
Above the sea blue,
Connects two sides
with different culture view
and making everyone
to think for you.
With your famous center
Top Capi Saray.
You are like magnet,
every tourist can go
and again is coming back
with your magical shopping center
in Aksaray appears through
all the tourists are in love with you.
With your nature and architecture,
Istanbul you are so beautiful.
The different languages, that are
speaking in your heart.
for people Istanbul you are light,
so lovely and wonderful.

Lovely September.

Every time that September is coming
I feel myself very joyful.
I will use my tradition
to be in my dearest country,
Albania that is so beautiful.
Everyday I enjoy this vacation,
With friends of mine,
that are coming from Europe
for our lovely meeting in Tirana.
When we are talking and walking
like on a thick smooth carpet,
placed on sidewalk,
by the yellow leaves,
that are falling by the trees,
my heart is full with happiness.
I am watching a big changing
and my blood is moving fast
in my body through,
I feel happy myself
In my mind in my heart
Between child hood
and prospect hopeful
for Tirana that is magical city
and wonderful.
For this lovely time
I love you month of
September colorful.

Our Meeting.

I am thinking all the time
The moment that I will meet you.
I am preparing different words
To talk with you,
Some of them are coming easy out,
Some of them are staying inside too.
I am confuse which words to use
to be helpful,
that our communication
to be wonderful.
But all the words that are coming
From my heart are so true.
It is a long time that I am waiting,
This moment to come
and to be hopeful,
to bring more clarity and establish
feelings between me and you.
I am waiting full with happiness and
my emotions are coming through.
I want this meeting
To be blessed with glory for my best
and hot feelings that I have for you.
I am thinking so much for this lovely
meeting named you.

Between Desperate and Love.

The weather looks so gray.

The white clouds do not appear

In the sky that erased its smile bright.

The raining is coming down and is washing

The green cover by the trees and grass

On the land around.

Like the raining,

the tears are coming down

to my face and heart is full with sadness.

I do not know why in

this moment so desperate,

I am thinking so much for you.

My thoughts are mixer

with desperate and love,

when in front of me I imagen you,.

In my soul's weather cold,

Your image is like a small sun

That makes my heart warm.

While I am swimming

in trouble water through,

I am thinking so much for you,

I feel that I love you.

We love you Amanda.

Amanda you are so sweet
With your face very white
And your hair color gold
Your smile is so warm.
With your eyes very blue
Your beauty is so true.
When you are talking with us
with your melodious voice
our happiness is the most.
Little Amanda you are so beautiful,
When you are coming to visit us,
our house looks so wonderful.
Our lovely niece
with your sweet words
and your smile, you are giving
to us a happy time.
Our dear Amanda,
Your face is so beautiful,
your conversation is so wonderful
your presence between us
is bringing happiness through
for all of them we love you.

I want to Say Excuse!

Never I knew how much I love you,
Only when far away from me was you.
How much I asked everyone for you.
How many states in Europe
searched for you.
I needed so much to speak with you,
to go out of this situation blue.
Our communication for me
has a big value.
I can't afford my suffering
and my lonely without you.
I can't find what part of my speech
hurts so much you
and brought between us
freeze situation through.
Slowly, slowly around the Europe
came the weather cold
and I am fighting with my thoughts.
I am traveling faraway again
To wait in the future
to come the sun
our communication to be warm.
I want to say excuse to you
And to tell truly
how much I love you

Your Writing.

I am waiting every time
Your writing to give me
Light and peace in my mind.
My sweet feelings are
blooming up
When I am reading through,
My thoughts are concentrating to you
and vibration waves
are creating between me and you.
Some times your writing
I do not understand but
when they are missing
I feel myself bad.
Like interrogatory is starting
a strong battle to myself.
My different and confuse
Thoughts are moving fast
When conflict signals
I see in our communication
In this solid bridge between us.
More establish and warm
in your writing in time
in my feeling
will be more harmony and light.

I love Los Angeles.

A trip down of memory lane
is just pleasure for me today
as the first place that I landed in U. S
you are important in my heart
beautiful Los Angeles.
Your peace advertise
"The Peace and Hope"
Also
"Angeles' Land"
It is watching by everyone
that is very lovely for immigrants.
I lived a beautiful time
On one quiet corner
Under the hill
that ended to Yucca street.
With welcome to a lot tourists

A lot museums and theaters
are standing proudly
with boulevard Sunset
very long and wide,
that make you beautiful
Hollywood Highland.
Your famous name
is granted by super stars,
and studio Universal also
by hope that you are giving
to people around.
I love you as the first place
that I came in U. S,
my mind and my heart
every time is coming back to you
Los Angeles.

Day of Betrayel.

Is coming day of anniversary
Across the spring time,
when you promised
me the "Big Love"
was the wonderful day
with your words of hot love
that the winter ice turned
to the water of spring time
and my life was so bright.
With your magical smile
My heart was not more quiet.
For you I gave a mountain
With love during this time.
Suddenly some signals like
black clouds arrived to my heart,
for answer I received your betrayal
"Changed Mind".

Your love was only with words
not with heart
Our love was for you one game
That broke my heart.
Now I am strong and quiet
In this anniversary,
I have the clear mind
that during the life between
the wonderful days of love
happens to have and days
named "Betrayal"

City College.

I want to sing one song for you.
City College I came to you
For knowledge.
I was thinking for a long time before
To study for Associate degree
and Bachelor.
Your place is lighting by knowledge.
I learned about life in this planet
By Living Environment.
I studied the Law that protects
the people in their life and property
by due Process.
Was interesting about career
of employee in Business Strategy
the most important for me
The America Government history.
City College in my memories
you are bright,
people with your knowledge
are improving their life.
In your international student community
Everyone is proud member to be.
For all emotions and knowledge,
That I have from you, as your student
I am saying to you:
City college Thank you.

Survey.

I am working day and night
I am tired to win the prize.
I am trying to learn more and more
I am learning to love you software.
During answer to the questions
of this survey.
I know now more companies
In their different ways.
I am waiting and playing in this
Strange Survey.
I lost my energy and my time
I waste but I won knowledges
in different ways.
My mind is working hard.
Numbers and names are
running fast.
The computer's screen
shows name of each company,
at the last as always
won you survey.
Thank you survey
for your impression,
thank you survey
for your information

Winter Cold Day

It was one winter cold day
We stood in front face to face
Around only ice and snow we saw
While my hands in your hands
felt warm,
from the moment to moment
lovely feelings appeared to blow.
Through to the white panorama
In your eyes I saw one
mountain with love.
Together we started to talk
while the air warm from our breath
was flying up with flocks of snow
while stamped the big sign of love
to the glasses of the building's window.
I was happy for my love
that found support to you,
I thought this feeling of love
will be bright as in winter
and summer time.
It was one beautiful white
winter cold day,
I talked and laughed with you,
While our love and happiness
flew up with flock of snow
to the sky blue,
I was happy to stay with you.

I see you soon!

A long time ago we said each other
with tears in our eyes and nostalgia
I will see you soon.
The plane was flying up
and gave to our life
different direction and sides.
I felt pain, never my tears stopped
coming down to my face.
The trip was so long
as my line of memories
with my heart was doing test
I thought you for all my life
and I found that my heart
was so glad.
I am very happy
for my lovely secret.
We tried to our life in different ways.
We believed in supreme power
An ultimate way,
To change the course of things
And to make our life
the reflection of our
most best desires
and wonderful dreams.
After the long time I understood,
how much I need and love
this phrase so powerful,
I see you soon.

The Reason I Do not Know.

I hoped so much in your helping.

I was so wrong in my waiting

I gave a lot information about case,

And I received strangely

one death silence

I am confuse about my thoughts,

I am confuse about my doubts.

I waited solution by you

That practice the law.

I want to establish

my different ideas

about your behavior,

but about my choice,

I do not know.

It is your mind and your heart

frozen by steel's frame of the law?

Or are other sources

about your "frozen"

and "death silence"

that I do not know.

Whatever reason it must to be

One answer reason must exist

between you and me.

The powerful of life's law is

Communication Key.

My Hesitation to Act.

With my thoughts of my mind
I decided to put you out.
With my feelings of my heart
Always you are part of my life.
No one fully understand
the ways of the heart,
so and for me is difficult
this mixer situation to delight
some feeling make me sad
some feelings makes me glad.
All these feelings conglomerate
Are giving me hesitation to act.
Inside my heart is strong weather
with rain, wind, sun very hot,
that day to day
shown various fun and fight.
About you I want to put
peace in my mind and
calm situation to my heart.
To go faraway that radar
does not accepts your waves
is the most loyal and best way.

Wild Separate.

In this moment with full silence
The bad words I remembered
That place for love never left.
Both of us our love story
we gave end.
I tried to remember
the beautiful moments in this silence
but the deadly cloud I experienced
from the poison of your badly words.
After our beautiful story
we are not anymore good friends,
we separate through our hearts
are weighing a full hate.
We fought each other
with words very bad
in this " Wild Separate"
we did no find one more easy way
to say to each other " Farewell ".
we loved we fought,
we hated each other in terrible way
like quickly strong storm weather,
that sent us forever faraway.
But I am waiting one rainbow
to give peace in our heart anyway.

Sunday Our Argue.

A long time I am with you.
Like clear water our life
was going through.
A long time I am with you,
A long time I was enjoying
my happiness too.
Something change to you and
all this time we have argue.
Something changed last time
that made to start the fight
of my thought with diversity in my mind.
What happened with you
that made me not to sleep
While all the night I think?
Every day and night to argue with you,
I am not quiet
I am looking for explanation everywhere
You made for me without spring this year.
The four seasons you made with snow,
And our love was going with flow.
In your heart if I have place anymore,
I do not know.

Mixer in Our Love Story.

One bird is singing the song.
On the tree I am hearing by my window
Very quietly,
while my thoughts flew
to my beautiful youngest time.
My memories are bringing
in front of me our meeting
on the park full with trees
where the birds were singing
the song for you and me.
You was reading with passion
some poems.
I was repeating the table
of Mendelejev.
Nervous all the time you argued
While I mixed Physic and Chemistry
In our meeting of our love story.
Always lovely I said to you,
because of my restriction
in biography, I must to study
very hard to win to study University.
So a long time was continuing
This big mixer,
your Poems, Physic and Chemistry
in our beautiful love story.

My Lovely Day

I am happy with Euphoria
I want everyone to be like me.
All the worries I left on side
Today I am thinking my
happiness to be so long,
my thoughts are flying hot.
I want that friends of mine
to enjoy that day that I love.
Everyone has in this time
one special day that gives fun.
My lovely day is giving
so much energy,
to fulfill the best wishes for me.
So for me this day will be far away
from desperate and anxiety.
It will be full with love peace and laugh,
And to make my life light.
I will give today to everyone love
And the flowers that are blooming
On the green grass, and the birds that
Are signing song on the trees,
I want all this nature around to be
Happy like me.

Your Golden Friendship.

I am sure this all comes
like surprise to you,
what I want to tell to you,
for my inspiration is coming through
and you want to ask
whom this hope is coming from?
that makes my feelings so strong.
It is your hand and your support,
That makes me strong.
It is your golden friendship
That makes alive our relationship.
It is your life, it is your joke
during my difficult time
caused to give up, turned me on,

erased my failure,
and is awaking my smile,
I love your optimism that
gave to me positive energy,
I love your laughing,
I love your smile,
That are lighting my mind.
That are shaking down
my failure and desperate,
that are sending my sadness faraway.
And to my success are opening way.
I want to be for a long time
with your laughing and your smile.
and our golden friendship to be alive.

Changing Season.

Slowly time by time day by day,

The sun is reducing its warm

and its rays are not very hot,

above me the leaves of the trees

are starting to fall down on the street.

My hearts is feeling

that very soon

the Autumn will meet.

The cheers of the children

are sounding everywhere,

their books to buy,

for one new year school to prepare.

Shown me that Autumn season

proudly is coming soon everywhere.

The people are changing their clothes

of summer time

with more warmer clothes

and said to Autumn season

one sweet welcome.

With all these changing

of the people activity

and their clothes with diversity,

nature looks so wonderful,

the Autumn is coming so beautiful.

WAR

One child asked his father:
What is the meaning war?
Father answered so short:
There are some reasons
that war is happening for.
What kind of reasons are bringing
The war everywhere?
Are good reasons for that.
What are good reasons
that are bringing death?
That can destroy everything
on this Earth?!
That are bringing a lot fears all the times,
that are taking a lot lives.
Father answered with deep thoughts.
Some wars are for democracy.

Some wars are for properties
Some wars for independence
And some others wars for you
and me never we can understand.
Now that science is in progress
For this matter dialog- communication
does not accepts.
The child confuse said:
This difficult term
I can't understand,
your explanation about war,
but for me has meaning only Terror.
Today in modern society
dialog must be Honor.

Kosovo's War.

My memories are bringing
In front of my eyes
A difficult time
When Albanian people
Suffered a terrible war
By other people with their head hot.
I remember now in silence
Those people with their eyes
full with tears,
that thought their lands, houses, behind,
that lost their dreams.
From this terrible war
The flowers covered all around the fields
They are honor of blood of martyrs of life,
for their Kosovo must to be pride.
These beautiful flowers are giving full color
While are erasing the dark of the war.

I remember the missioner of Peace
That gave to you again full fill dream.
Now you are changing fast
Beautiful Kosovo,
your improving wounded
are sing of life,
that you are spreading
all around the world,
while on those field
the flowers multicolor
are giving to you the color of life
to erase the dark of the war.

Faith.

I thought all day long,
What is more important word
In dictionary,
to make more strong
our relationship between you and me.
Hours and hours I was reading
Different pages in my dictionary
And the words were flying
with speed in front of me.
At last I found the small word
With big meaning for you and me.
FAITH…!
Faith this golden word as a bridge
that connects two souls,
must be engaged with loyalty.
With Faith I sense everything
is in harmony.
The relationship is peaceful
you and me will feel
serenely secure.
Without faith the life has not light,
no romantic relationship,
can live a long, no friendship can grow up.
Some faith in your inside,
your heart will be delight.

Mimoza.

I love the trees with flowers Mimoza
with yellow colors and wonderful aroma
that makes me warm.
I love the beautiful Mimoza
That were blooming everywhere
All around my lovely city Tirana
During February the month of love
With its Saint Valentine day.
I like their proudly blooming
With force with bright color,
In the heart and wild grey winter
with its cold and warm.
In this mosaic grey yellow and green,
I saw your challenging as you won,
Between cold weather and feeling warm.
I saw flowers of mimosa in hand of everyone
As symbol of love to my people in Tirana.
My favorite and beautiful Mimoza
I know your mission is strong and very hard,
To send love in every heart.
I love you every time and everywhere
As the first present of my love
of the Saint Valentine Day.

The flowers of May.

It was one time

Our feeling were with clarity

When we did not know the world "Hypocrisy"

It was one lovely spring day

You came to me with your smile

In your hand you held the flower of May.

All the colorful flowers

that were sprouting all over the place

had jealousy

when the flower of May you gave to me.

It was the secret lovely witness in our love story.

With your sweet words you kissed me

I felt warm.

The kiss was mixer with wonderful aroma

At time my heart spoke with great love and joy.

The leaves of the trees were moving slowly,

This view enjoyed.

The birds of the trees they started their song

They sent to us their love support.

Forever I love the Flower of May

That remember me the lovely time.

Lily Flower.

You beautiful Lily Flowers
you kindly that smelling
are spreading around
and shown to nature that
you are preferred by everyone,
because your name is used
and by people that make
you so proud.
Lily flower your name is well known
for your beauty color
people your name are using
like honor.
I love the flowers Lily
where are blooming
on wide field through
the green grass,
while are creating one
beautiful image.

I like Lily flowers' color
in different clothes
that looks so bright
when people are using
during spring time.
Dear Lily flowers for your beauty color
that appears to name of people,
to different clothes and nature around,
it is so magnificent in this conglomerate
you are giving to people happiness
in spring time.

I do not want to lose you.

With your action I judged you.
I thought that with your losing,
The beautiful things I am losing too.
I lose the beautiful time that
I was thinking for you.
I lose my good feelings
To buy presents for you
and to enjoy your reaction
about them, what you are thinking too.
I lose my hope to enjoy some moments
when I am seeing and meeting you
while the glad was filling my heart through.
I lose my writing that I sent to you,
through them I was telling my daily life
most of it I was thinking for you.
So with all those losing
I lose my happy moments that filled my life
with happiness and fun too,
so as my big wish is to enjoy
all these beautiful things through
I do not want to lose you!

I Love Your Changing.

Every day I see big changing
In your behavior
that makes my heart warm.
Every day I see your kindly
Talking to me that makes
My soul quiet to be.
Every time I feel more better
Communication between
You and me that makes
daily life so happy.
I think and I feel that our
Relationship is taking color bright
Looks that between us will come
the warm spring time.
I love this warm,
I like this color bright,
I love this situation is becoming hot
That put us together very close.
I like all these changing around you
That are creating one big clue.
I love this warm, I love this color bright,
I love this communication hot
That is coming through,
because I Love You.

81 Spring Time.

I am happy today and I see
The beautiful flowers around
are happy like me.
I am happy today and I see
That with wonderful songs,
the birds on the trees
are happy like me,
I am walking on sidewalk,
And enjoying this beauty of nature.
I feel that proudly Palmas
are looking to me.
They want to know my euphoria.
The green grass carpet
with his silence,
for my joyful has a big curiosity.

The golden sun with his rays
is touching my skin with jealousy,
with his provocative warm wants
attention of me
as always winner of my feelings
it wants to be.
My heart is full with love and joy.
I love this nature that is giving hope,
sense, energy, how to live in harmony,
with those that are close to me.
I am telling all of them secret of mine,
Today I am in love with spring time.

82 Jealousy.

I loved your face and your smile
Like spring's flowers
Were blooming my happy life.
Suddenly as black cloud
Through sunny day,
Came to my heart jealousy
At luxury restaurant you and me
Were celebrating our anniversary.
With your magical words
That like butterflies flew to me
With musical sounds very lovely,
Through the red wine's glass
In your hand,
I saw how you looked at her
For my love I felt pain.
You broke my heart
You broke my sweet dream,
For my love's story
I have nostalgia,
It was true love
between you and me.

Love.

I wrote to you for my love
I waited answer for a long time
I thought every day,
I dreamed every night
For your answer
to give me some light
in my heart.
Hours days and nights I passed,
With thinking and dreaming for
Your "answer love".
I asked myself:
It is fair,
To wait and to think
for somebody,
That for my love
does not show interest?!
Now my heart is cold,
My heart is fresh,
I want to save my heart,
my mind and my time
for more important event
at last your answer came,
it was for me like Rudiment

Beach of Adriatic Sea,

A long line of the beach
of Adriatic sea
with is wonderful view
and its water color blue
that Albania can be proud too.
The blue color sea
from the white waves
Is taking light garniture
Beautiful design ensure
From the wind is going up
to the hill to meet color green
and so many monuments' historic
that are making this beach
very interesting.

Around the fields with their
flowers colorful
that are watching in silence
this panorama beautiful
are trees at all
that are creating one
frame honor.
White houses with red roof
all around
for their beauty architecture
are standing proud
Between hills and Adriatic sea,
Color mosaic, magnificent view
Everyone can see.

Our Favorite place

Every time each other
We met with euphoria,
to our favorite place
to lake on the hill.
We were playing
and running so fast
We talked and laughed so much,
never we felt that
was going quickly the time,
while our thoughts
were flying with wind.
All people around
that walked on this hill
with that deep lake blue
watched very strangely
for me and you.

They can't understood
our happiness too.
From routine of our office
on this beautiful place
with its deep lake blue on the hill
we felt ourselves free
the most happy time for you and me.
I want to be again on this
blue lake on the hill,
on this beautiful place I want to be,
From my worries,
I want myself to feel free
While to remember this beautiful
time for you and me.

Beautiful Ksamil

During the long beach of
The very blue Jon sea,
The beautiful Ksamil
everyone will see.
Orange and Limone
in wide plantation
on the hills around the sea
are creating one frame
very green.
From Greek Island Corfuse
Through the Jon sea is coming
one wind full with jealousy.
Ksamil with his view
very peaceful is sending
messages by the tourists
to island Corfuse,
like you I am so beautiful
also people are making
my view wonderful
with modern architecture.
For my land, I feel proud to be,
Like Greek Famous Achropoli,
I have in my heart famous
Amphitheater of beautiful Butrint
That is very lovely for all,
Archelogy and tourists
So like you they will love and me

Flowers Of Garden.

Under the sun rays
The flowers are opening petals
And their colors looks so bright.
Every flowers feels its duty
In this garden to show their beauty.
The first started the white rose.
I am so beautiful my white color
Is giving peace to everyone
that it needs.
The red rose shows capricious,
Because red color is color of Love,
That its red color is very important
of everyone.
Suddenly moved petals Lily Flower,
hey all of you know the fact,
that people are using my name
for themselves because
so much me, they love.
Under the warm sun,
its color is so light
of the Flower Butterfly.

Everyone loves my beauty,
To shown my beauty
It is my duty.
When I am opening my petals
under dear hot sun,
my colors petals looks like in fly
of the wings of butterfly.
The Garden shown so powerful,
for its treasure collection
of these flowers so beautiful
that give to everyone one
view wonderful.

Evening On The Beach!

At the evening on the beach
I was losing in my dream
for faraway to my country.
I was watching to the east
when the blue color of ocean
become together in one line
with light blue of the sky.
Slowly the golden sun with silence
Is going away to be hidden
through the clouds faraway.
Some white Pelicans
above water of ocean.
started their flying
and gave their greeting
to me of Good night.
The waves are coming with noise
like circle white
above blue water of ocean,
while silver moon is sending
its light proudly above the ocean,
it wants to give support
to my thoughts for my country
and friends of mine.

My Battle

I wrote all the time about you
I want your brain's acceptors
To get my feelings through.
Sometimes I tried to stop my hand
To write to you,
But my heart blamed too.
My mind in instinctively way
Gave signals about you.
A long time I have this battle
with my heart.
My hands tried to stop
but my heart pushed it
for you to write.
But my mind shown
proudly her brain so powerful,
that gave statement
without me you never can decide too,
I am power for both of you.
So I left myself under the blessing
Of the powerful of protection
of my mind, to decide
and to put in resonance with my hand
and my heart,
for you to stop or to write.

I Can't Love Bankruptcy.

Every time I argued with friends of mine,
How to establish our problems in line.
Some justified with acknowledges,
Some said was a law interest,
About our business.
So they found one very short way
to get off problem from our heads,
And to give one honor place to our silence
for those difficult things for them and for me
only one way is to sign Bankruptcy.
I know you bankruptcy
you have a big heart,
you try to save for different people
their situation very hard.
Your term is open around so wide,
Your importance is so light,
But your bright I do not like.
I want to say so sorry to you,
bankruptcy I accept your existence
and your helping too,
but I can't love you.

Fourth of July Celebration!

Firelights are breaking my silence
while are giving different colors
Up to the sky that has dressed
The dark veil of the night
And the stars are brighten light.
On different squares,
All people are celebrating
Fourth of July, big holiday
full of joy and happiness.
It is anniversary of each year
of big success
of Americans' modern life
that is giving to everyone
one big smile.
It is glory of the music, and science,
it is planting of the land and
build buildings in sky limit,
turning the dream in reality
in infinity.
The Fourth July the beautiful present
heritage by famous and smart men,
and brave people,
that with their mind and their blood
made Fourth July Legend
forever to shine with color bright.

The Moment Has Arrived.

The moment has arrived
to show to you,
truly how I am feeling about
your speech with different meaning.
I can't change your behavior
and your way of thinking.
I can't change your capricious
mind for our feelings,
but I can try,
to get help by Universe
about my dreaming
and to improve myself
and my thinking.
The moment has arrived
to leave you quiet
with your selfish lovely thinking,
to enjoy your capricious juicy feelings.
I feel strong and more quiet
myself now about my feelings.
I see very clear in this world
there are a lot beautiful things
and good people,
with them I will achieve my
"Dreaming".